EARLY PEOPLES

PEOPLES OF THE ARCTIC AND SUBARCTIC

WORLD
BOOK

World Book
a Scott Fetzer company
Chicago
www.worldbookonline.com

World Book, Inc.
233 N. Michigan Avenue
Chicago, IL 60601
U.S.A.

For information about other World Book publications, visit our Web site at **http://www.worldbookonline.com** or call **1-800-WORLDBK (967-5325)**.
For information about sales to schools and libraries, call **1-800-975-3250 (United States)**, or **1-800-837-5365 (Canada)**.

Library of Congress Cataloging-in-Publication Data

Peoples of the Arctic and Subarctic.
    p. cm. -- (Early peoples)
   Includes index.
   Summary: "A discussion of the Indians of the Arctic and Subarctic regions of North America, including who the people were, where they lived, their civilization, social structure, religion, art, architecture, science and technology, daily life, entertainment and sports. Features include timelines, fact boxes, glossary, list of recommended readings, web sites, and index"--Provided by publisher.
   ISBN 978-0-7166-2132-4
   1. Paleo-Eskimos--Arctic regions--History--Juvenile literature. 2. Paleo-Eskimos--Arctic regions--Social life and customs--Juvenile literature. 3. Inuit--Arctic regions--History--Juvenile literature. 4. Inuit--Arctic regions--Social life and customs--Juvenile literature. 5. Indians of North America--Arctic regions--History--Juvenile literature. 6. Indians of North America--Arctic regions--Social life and customs--Juvenile literature. 7. Arctic regions--Social life and customs. I. World Book, Inc.
E99.E7P347 2009
971.9'01--dc22
                                    2008040637

Printed in China
1 2 3 4 5 13 12 11 10 09

STAFF

EXECUTIVE COMMITTEE
President
 Paul A. Gazzolo
Vice President and Chief Marketing Officer
 Patricia Ginnis
Vice President and Chief Financial Officer
 Donald D. Keller
Vice President and Editor in Chief
 Paul A. Kobasa
Director, Human Resources
 Bev Ecker
Chief Technology Officer
 Tim Hardy
Managing Director, International
 Benjamin Hinton

EDITORIAL
Editor in Chief
 Paul A. Kobasa
Associate Director, Supplementary Publications
 Scott Thomas
Managing Editor, Supplementary Publications
 Barbara A. Mayes
Senior Editor, Supplementary Publications
 Kristina Vaicikonis
Manager, Research, Supplementary Publications
 Cheryl Graham
Manager, Contracts & Compliance
 (Rights & Permissions)
 Loranne K. Shields

Administrative Assistant
 Ethel Matthews
Editors
 Nicholas Kilzer
 Scott Richardson
 Christine Sullivan

GRAPHICS AND DESIGN
Associate Director
 Sandra M. Dyrlund
Manager
 Tom Evans
Coordinator, Design Development and Production
 Brenda B. Tropinski

EDITORIAL ADMINISTRATION
Director, Systems and Projects
 Tony Tills
Senior Manager, Publishing Operations
 Timothy Falk

PRODUCTION
Director, Manufacturing and Pre-Press
 Carma Fazio
Manufacturing Manager
 Steve Hueppchen
Production/Technology Manager
 Anne Fritzinger
Production Specialist
 Curley Hunter
Proofreader
 Emilie Schrage

MARKETING
Chief Marketing Officer
 Patricia Ginnis
Associate Director, School and Library Marketing
 Jennifer Parello

Produced for World Book by
White-Thomson Publishing Ltd.
+44 (0)845 362 8240
www.wtpub.co.uk
Steve White-Thomson, President

Writer: Barbara Davis
Editor: Robert Famighetti
Designer: Clare Nicholas
Photo Researcher: Amy Sparks
Map Artist: Stefan Chabluk
Illustrator: Adam Hook (p. 39)
Fact Checker: Chelsey Hankins
Proofreader: Kelly Davis
Indexer: Nila Glikin

Consultant:
Robert McGhee
Curator of Western Arctic Archaeology
Canadian Museum of Civilization
Hull, Quebec, Canada

TABLE OF CONTENTS

Glossary There is a glossary on pages 60-61. Terms defined in the glossary are in type **that looks like this** on their first appearance on any spread (two facing pages).

Additional Resources Books for further reading and recommended Web sites are listed on page 62. Because of the nature of the Internet, some Web site addresses may have changed since publication. The publisher has no responsibility for any such changes or for the content of cited sources.

WHO WERE THE PEOPLES OF THE ARCTIC AND SUBARCTIC?

The Arctic and Subarctic regions that make up the northernmost part of North America are some of the harshest environments in the world. Despite this, people have lived in these areas for thousands of years. Populations were never very large. In fact, even today the Subarctic region has fewer people living in it per square mile than any other populated area in the world. It is clear that the peoples of the Arctic and Subarctic were, and are, among the hardiest on Earth.

The peoples of the Arctic and Subarctic originally came from Asia, **migrating** over many thousands of years. They were hunters and fishers. Indians of the Subarctic were the first people to live in North America. Some of their descendants traveled much farther south and east in North America and into South America.

Enduring Traditions

Those who stayed in the Arctic and Subarctic learned to live with the constant struggle to stay warm and to find food. They made the most of the available resources, devising tools and ways of life that have endured to the present day.

▼ The two areas where the Arctic and Subarctic peoples live cover most of the northernmost regions of North America—regions where winter temperatures can drop below -75 °F (-60 °C).

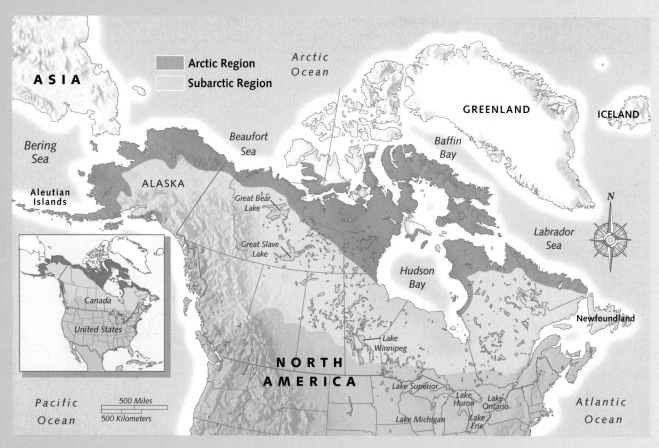

The Subarctic was mostly occupied by Indians from two major language families and with different histories. In the eastern and central Subarctic, people who spoke the Algonquian *(al GONG kee uhn)* languages flourished. The Cree became the most numerous of the eastern Subarctic Indians, forming subgroups such as the Western Wood Cree, Swampy Cree, and Mistassini *(mihs TIHS uh nee)* Cree.

People speaking Athabaskan *(ath uh BAS kuhn)* languages settled in the western part of the Subarctic. They lived throughout what is now northwestern Canada and central Alaska. The tribes within this area of the Subarctic developed diverse traditions and ways of life. Some, like the Carrier and Chilcotin *(chihl KOH tihn)*, were influenced by neighboring Indian tribes of the Northwest Coast. The Chipewyan *(CHIHP uh WY uhn)* and Beaver tribes were influenced by their neighbors to the east, the Cree.

The Inuit *(IHN yu iht)*, or Eskimos, are the people of the Arctic. They are not related to North American Indians, including the Indians of the Subarctic. The Inuit share ancestors with the Aleuts *(AL ee ootz)* of the Aleutian *(uh LOO shuhn)* Islands, located southwest of what is now Alaska. These ancestors came from northeast Asia. Inuit language and **culture** are notably different from those of the North American Indians and the people of the Subarctic.

WHAT IS IN A NAME?

At one time, the Arctic people were called Eskimos. To some of these people, Eskimo was an insulting name because it is an Indian word that was thought to mean *eater of raw meat.* Many Arctic people prefer the term "Inuit," which means *the people.* "Inuk" is the singular form of Inuit and means *person.* Even though Inuit is now the more commonly used name to describe Arctic people, there are still some groups in Alaska who refer to themselves as Eskimos.

◀ An Inuit woman, photographed in the early 1900's. The Inuit are the native people of the Arctic region. Living in one of the harshest climates on Earth, they were creative in how they used the resources available to them—especially a wealth of fur-bearing sea and land animals that provided them with food and the warm clothing necessary to survive.

Origins and Migrations

Scholars know little about the first Americans. Their story begins thousands of years ago. Scientists called **archaeologists** *(AHR kee OL uh jihstz)* have used such clues as stone tools and animal and human bones to learn how and when these earliest peoples lived.

Origins of the Subarctic Indians

Archaeologists believe the first people may have arrived in the region near Alaska as early as 30,000 years ago, during the last **ice age**. These ancestors of the American Indians were hunters from northeastern Asia. They journeyed east, following game animals across the land. Sea levels were lower during the last ice age, because of the vast amounts of water locked into glaciers, and people were able to walk across what is now the floor of the Bering Sea. They found themselves in a new homeland in what is now Alaska. This was the first area of the Americas to be inhabited. Initially, they could not venture further because the land was covered with huge ice sheets. Over time, some of their descendants **migrated** to populate the entire continents of North America and South America. From about 15,000 years ago, Indians spread east and south from Alaska to occupy all of the Subarctic region and the rest of the Americas.

▲ An artist's depiction of hunters from Asia traveling to Alaska tens of thousands of years ago during the last ice age. Because so much of Earth's water was locked up in vast ice sheets and sea levels were lower, these hunters were able to walk across what is now the Bering Sea. They became the first people to live in North America.

Origins of the Arctic Peoples

The people of the Arctic are not Indians and have a different ancestry from the Subarctic Indians. About 5,000 years ago, new settlers from Asia arrived in North America. They came in small boats or walked over frozen seas in winter. They made their way to what is now Alaska and the Canadian Arctic. Historians call these non-Indian migrants Paleo-Eskimos. They were the first people to live in the Arctic region year-round. The Paleo-Eskimos lived in North America until about 1,000 years ago.

The ancestors of the Inuit and Aleut peoples, who also came from Asia, have lived on the Aleutian Islands and the Pacific coast of Alaska since about 10,000 years ago. About 2,000 years ago, Inuit people moved northward around the coast of Alaska; by about 1,000 years ago, they occupied most of the Canadian Arctic and Greenland. For a time, Paleo-Eskimo and Inuit groups lived in the same areas. Eventually, the Paleo-Eskimos died out, and the Inuit remained. The Inuit continue to live in the Arctic today.

TIMELINE OF THE ARCTIC AND SUBARCTIC PEOPLES

30,000 years ago – People from northeastern Asia move into the region around the Bering Sea and later cross into what is now Alaska.

15,000 years ago – The people living in Alaska begin to move south and east and populate other areas of North and South America.

12,000–8,000 years ago – Indians moving east from Alaska occupy all of the Subarctic.

5,000 years ago – new settlers from northeastern Asia arrive in North America. These people are known as Paleo-Eskimos.

2,000 years ago – Inuit begin moving northward around coastal Alaska.

1,000 years ago – Inuit have moved into the Canadian Arctic and Greenland. Paleo-Eskimos die out.

◄ Fragments of flint drills, blades, and scrapers found in the Arctic dating from about 3000 to 2000 B.C. The early peoples of the Arctic knew that flint, a hard rock, could be shaped into durable and very sharp tools. Most of these tools are no more than 2 inches (5 centimeters) long and required great skill to make.

CHALLENGE OF THE FAR NORTH

Although the Arctic and Subarctic might appear to be vast empty spaces, to the hunting peoples of the Arctic and Subarctic, the areas were rich in resources they could use successfully.

Land of the Midnight Sun

The Arctic region of North America extends for 5,000 miles (8,000 kilometers) from west to east—from Alaska across the northernmost parts of Canada to northern Greenland. This is an area of craggy coastlines, islands, and expanses of flat, treeless, frozen land called **tundra** *(TUHN druh)*. It is an extreme environment. Winters are long, cold, and dark. At the height of winter, there are only a few hours of daylight each day. In the northernmost areas, the sun is not seen at all for more than four months. During these times of darkness, temperatures can drop below -75 °F (-60 °C).

In spring and summer, the situation changes. Warmer temperatures cause the ice to break up both on land and on the water. In places where the sun is essentially not seen in the winter, it is seen almost all the time in summer. During

WORDS FOR SNOW

For the Inuit, snow conditions were a matter of life and death. If the snow was heavy and the wind was high, snowdrifts might bury footprints and animal tracks, and a hunter could get lost. As a result, the Inuit became experts in—and developed many ways to describe—different types of snow. They have a few root words for different kinds of snow, to which various descriptive terms are added to form an almost endless number of compound words to describe varieties of snow conditions. For example, qaniqsineq *(kah neek see nehk)* is a word that describes snow floating on water; muruaneq *(moo roo ah nehk)* is a soft and deep snow. It is a common misconception that the Inuit have dozens or hundreds of different words for snow. In fact, English and Inuit have around the same number of root words for snow.

some days, the sky never really darkens, even at midnight. For this reason, the northern Arctic is called the "land of the midnight sun." The constant sunlight can cause temperatures to reach as high as 85 °F (30 °C).

In the tundra, **permafrost**—ground that remains frozen for two or more years at a time—limits the growth of plant roots and tends to keep water close to the surface. Therefore, trees cannot grow on it. However, above the permafrost, a layer of soil about 1.5 to 16.5 feet (0.5 to 5 meters) thick freezes and thaws enough to permit low-lying bushes, grasses, and wildflowers to grow. In the summer, the tundra comes alive with such plants as Arctic willow, crowberry, dwarf Arctic birch, and dwarf blueberry.

The Arctic is very dry. Only 2 to 10 inches (5 to 25 centimeters) of precipitation falls each year in most of the Arctic. Precipitation is usually in the form of snow. Parts of the Arctic are as dry as deserts are in other parts of the world.

A Special Kind of Wealth

To people who depended on animals to survive, the Arctic was anything but barren. The melting sea ice opens up waterways, and the natural **migration** patterns of certain animals cause them to gather in large groups during the Arctic summer. Large concentrations of caribou *(KAR uh boo)*, seals, walruses, and whales make them easy to find and hunt. Huge flocks of migratory birds head north to the tundra for the summer—there is ample food, and there are few predators for the birds to fear. The unfrozen rivers support dense populations of such fish as char, a type of trout. When the weather turns cold, all the food that the people have managed to gather from hunting and fishing can be safely frozen and stored to feed them throughout the coming dark winter.

▼ Caribou graze in the Canadian Arctic. During the short summer, the Arctic tundra comes alive with low-lying shrubs, wildflowers, and other plants. These plants provide food for migrating caribou that move north in huge numbers for the summer months. For the Arctic peoples, the annual caribou migration was a time to hunt. Meat and skins acquired during the summer would give the people food, clothing, and shelter during the long Arctic winter.

THE TAIGA

The Subarctic region stretches across the entire North American continent from Cook Inlet on the Pacific coast in the west to Newfoundland and the Gulf of St. Lawrence in the east. Its northern edge borders much of Hudson Bay, and its southeastern corner touches the north shore of Lake Superior. This huge geographic area covers most of present-day Canada and the central, or interior, part of Alaska—an area of about 2 million square miles (5 million square kilometers).

Tundra vs. Taiga

On the northern edge of the Subarctic, the landscape is similar to Arctic **tundra**. Farther south the land becomes **taiga** *(TY guh)*. The taiga, or boreal *(BAWR ee uhl)* forest, is a land of such evergreen trees as pine, fir, and spruce, and such **deciduous** *(dih SIHJ u uhs)* trees as aspen and birch. The ground is often spongy or swampy. Forests in the southern Subarctic are denser than those in the north. Ground-cover and berry bushes are also found on the taiga. Blueberry, high-bush cranberry, cloudberry, and rowan provide important food resources for animals and people.

▲ The major Indian tribes of the Subarctic are categorized by major language families—the Algonquian in the East and the Athabaskan in the West. Most tribes in the region that is now eastern and central Canada spoke Algonquian languages. The Cree in present-day Quebec, Ontario, Manitoba, and Saskatchewan were the most numerous of these. The area that is now western Canada and central Alaska was occupied for the most part by tribes speaking Athabaskan languages, including the Chipewyan in what is now northern Manitoba and Saskatchewan.

Much of the Subarctic gets far more precipitation than the Arctic region. Winters are long, cold, and harsh with a great deal of snow. In modern-day southwestern Ontario, Canada, average annual snowfall can be about 37 inches (94 centimeters). Farther east, annual snowfall can be more than 100 inches (254 centimeters). The ample precipitation supports large lakes, ponds, swamps, rivers, and streams. Three of the largest lakes in the world are located within the Subarctic region of North America—Great Bear Lake, Great Slave Lake, and Lake Winnipeg.

The summers are short and cool. For the most part, the people of the Subarctic depended on game animals for their food. Caribou **migrate** between the tundra and the taiga. The Chipewyan would follow those herds northward in spring and return to the forests in autumn. In other areas of the Subarctic, moose, musk oxen, and deer were abundant. Tribes such as the Tutchone *(too CHOHN ee)* that lived close to waterways fished for salmon, whitefish, or eels.

CLEANSING FIRE
Natural fires periodically swept through the dense stands of the taiga forest. A fire often started when lightning struck dry wood. Once started, the fire would jump from tree to tree and through the heavy brush that had collected under the trees over a period of years. These fires, while potentially disastrous, helped to clear away old growth and allow new plants and trees to grow. In this way, the natural fires helped the taiga forests to flourish and continue to be an all-important source of food and other resources for animals and people.

▼ The Subarctic taiga, or boreal forest, is covered with evergreen and deciduous trees and ground covers and grasses upon which moose, musk oxen, caribou, and deer feed. With plentiful annual rainfall, the taiga has numerous rivers, streams, and lakes, and much of the land is swampy.

INVENTIONS FROM THE PAST

Survival in a harsh climate was one of the greatest achievements of the Arctic and Subarctic peoples. They invented unique tools to help them live in their challenging environments. Versions of many of these tools are still used today.

Walking on Snow

People living in the Subarctic and Arctic were used to coping with long months of heavy snowfalls and snow-covered ground. Being able to travel through snow was a matter of survival. The most common way to travel was on foot. To make snow travel possible, both the Subarctic Indians and the Inuit used snowshoes made of bent wood frames and willow or rawhide webbing. The webbing would also have thongs to attach the snowshoes to winter **moccasins** *(MOK uh suhnz)* or boots.

Many tribes also had their own snowshoe designs. The Montagnais *(mahn tuhn YAY)* and Naskapi *(NAS kuh pee)* favored snowshoes that were almost round. Certain Cree tribes, on the other hand, crafted longer, narrower snowshoes. Some Cree hunters used snowshoes that were 7 to 8 feet (2 to 2.5 meters) long.

Regardless of design, snowshoes create a larger surface area that distributes the weight of a person stepping into snow. Therefore, the walker does not sink far into the snow with each step. It takes a lot of energy for a walker to repeatedly

▶ Snowshoes on display at Fort William, Ontario, a re-creation of a fur trading post in the Canadian Subarctic. Snowshoes were essential to both the Inuit and the Subarctic Indians, enabling them to track game over ground covered by heavy snow. Long, narrow snowshoes were often used in open areas with little brush. Shorter snowshoes were used in hilly country or for walking through woods. The shorter style made it easier to quickly turn or change direction, such as when following deer through the forest.

lift his or her foot out of deep snow. With snowshoes, the walker's feet stay closer to the surface of the snow, and the walker uses less energy. This was important to a hunter chasing caribou over miles and miles of open land.

High-Tech Harpoon

The Inuit invented a unique **harpoon** *(hahr POON)* to make it easier to kill whales, seals, and walruses (see page 38). When the harpoon was thrust into an animal, the **barbed** harpoon head hooked into its flesh, then twisted. This prevented the harpoon head from falling out as the animal tried to get away. The harpoon head then separated from the rest of the harpoon. Long thongs made out of animal skin connected the harpoon head to the bow of a boat. When the animal tired enough, the hunters might use the thongs to pull themselves closer to the animal. They could then use clubs to kill it. Or, if the animal died, the hunters could tow it back to the boat with the thongs. This high-tech harpoon was used by some of the earliest Arctic peoples.

▼ An Inuit man wears a pair of ivory snow goggles. The thin eye slits provide clear vision directly ahead and to the left and right. However, the opening is narrow enough to protect the hunter's eyes from the glare of sun on ice. The man holds an ivory pick with a long wooden handle that was used to travel safely over icy ground. A hunter drove the sharp point of the pick into the ice while using the handle for balance.

SNOW GOGGLES

The bright reflection of the sun off ice and snow can damage a person's eyesight, a serious problem for hunters who rely on keen eyesight to find food. The Inuit invented snow goggles to help them protect their vision. The goggles were made of ivory or wood and tied with thongs made of animal hide or tendons. The goggles had narrow slits that allowed the wearer to see out but prevented too much light from reaching the eyes. Even though they were a functional item, snow goggles could also be works of art. Many had beautiful carvings or other decorations.

ARCTIC AND SUBARCTIC SOCIETY

The Arctic and Subarctic make up a vast region where relatively few people lived. Many of these people spent a great deal of time moving from place to place in search of food. This frequent movement over a wide area led to an informal society made up of small groups. This allowed the people to adjust to changes in the amount of food that the land could provide.

Family

For most peoples of the Subarctic and Arctic, the family was the most important, and basic, group of society. A person identified first with his or her immediate family and other close relatives. The family would likely include a man and his wife, or wives, and all their unmarried children. Elderly relatives or unmarried relatives might also be part of this extended family.

Bands

A **band** was usually made up of a small number of families who were closely related. Among the Inuit, a band might include from 2 to 5 families, totaling up to about 25 people. Subarctic Indian bands included 2 to 12 families and ranged in size from about 25 to 100 people. Some bands, though, might have as many as 200 members. The number of people in a band depended on the resources available. If food was in short supply, the number of people in the band became smaller. Some members of the band might leave to join other bands, or the

▼ A photograph of an Inuit family in Nome, Alaska, taken in 1905. The individuals wear traditional caribou or sealskin parkas with fur-trimmed hoods. The family was the most important social group for the Arctic and Subarctic peoples and often included a man, his wife or wives, and their children, parents, and unmarried brothers and sisters.

Copyright 1905
F.H.Nowell
Nome

Alaska Eskimos

4402

▲ A Naskapi family photographed in Labrador, in eastern Canada, in the early 1920's. Such nontraditional clothing as the man's coat reflects the influence of modern society on the **cultures** of the Subarctic Indians.

very young or very old might die from lack of food. Each band lived and hunted in a defined area. Often the hunting area was shared with one or more other bands. Marriage and kinship strengthened the bonds between different bands sharing a hunting area.

Coming Together

Bands from specific regions that shared a common language and traditions constituted a tribe. The bands in a tribe typically came together at certain times of the year— for example, for large **communal** hunts during the summer or for such social events as seasonal ceremonies. These regional events could be attended by as many as 500 to 1,000 people.

STRUCTURED SOCIETIES

Unlike most other Arctic and Subarctic peoples, the Eastern Aleuts had a definite class system. Their system included *honorables*, who were of the highest rank. The next rank, *commoners*, included most of Aleut society. *Slaves* made up the lowest rank. The Aleuts' main loyalty was to the village rather than a band or tribe, and slaves were usually people who had been captured during raids on other villages. Honorables and commoners inherited their ranks, but the child of a slave would not necessarily also be a slave.

ROLES OF MEN AND WOMEN

▲ A Cree hunter blows a horn to attract a moose in a photograph from the 1920's. Hunting was one of the most important jobs for men among the Arctic and Subarctic peoples. The women, children, and older members of a **band** depended on the hunters' skills to provide them with food and the materials to make clothing and shelter.

The peoples of the Arctic and Subarctic divided most of the daily tasks of living between men and women. There were some tasks, however, performed by both. In some Subarctic tribes, both men and women looked after children. Making snowshoes was also a shared task. The men would make the snowshoe frames, and the women would weave the webbing. Regardless of a person's individual responsibilities, survival in a challenging environment required hard work from everyone.

A Man's Work

While women and children sometimes fished and snared rabbits or birds, men were responsible for hunting large game and for making the weapons they needed for the hunt. They also built the boats, sleds, and **toboggans** (tuh BOG uhnz) needed for transportation. Men prided themselves on their craftsmanship. Their skill was especially noticeable in the fine detailed carvings on such items as sewing needles, toys, and belt fasteners. These items were usually carved out of animal bone or antlers. In areas where the people lived in winter villages, the men built the larger shelters. This involved cutting wood and stripping bark to make log or plank frames. Cutting and stacking blocks of snow for snow houses was also considered a man's job. The heavy work of dragging whalebones for building houses also fell to the men and older boys.

A Woman's Work

A large part of a woman's work was centered on the home. This work included skinning and butchering the animals the men killed and cooking or preserving the meat. Women scraped the animal skins and then sewed them to make clothing and tents. Each home had a round pit circled with stones in which fires were lit for cooking and warmth. Women set up these pits and made sure the fire was kept burning. Among the Inuit, women chewed sealskin to make it soft enough to sew into clothing. Women also helped build shelters, especially the lighter shelters found in summer hunting or fishing camps. Like the men, the women excelled in their own fine craftsmanship, including detailed stitched decorations on clothing and sewn pouches.

ONE TOOL, MANY USES

Arctic women used a tool called an **ulu** *(OO loo)*. It was a curved and sharpened stone knife with a wood or bone handle. Different sizes of ulu were used for different tasks—everything from cutting and scraping animal skins to cutting frozen meat. It was also used during food preparation. The curved blade in the ulu at right is about 4 inches (10 centimeters) long and was used for cutting meat or removing **blubber** from skins. Smaller ulu, with blades about 2 inches (5 centimeters) long, were used to cut **sinew** *(SIHN yoo)* for sewing. The shape of the ulu causes the greatest force to be applied at the center of the blade. This makes it easier to cut through very hard substances such as animal bone. Although the ulu at right has an iron blade, traditional ulu made before the Inuit obtained iron from European traders had blades made of slate.

ONE WHO THINKS

The Inuit word *isumataq* (*ee soo mah tahk*) is used to describe a person in authority. It can be translated as *one who thinks.* This is a good description of one of the qualities the Arctic and Subarctic people looked for in a leader.

Temporary Position

Among most Arctic and Subarctic peoples, the leadership role was as informal and flexible as the society itself. The leader of a family or **band** changed depending on what was needed at a particular time. One person might act as a leader for a **communal** hunt; someone else might lead when a band decided to move within its territory. A successful whale hunter who had a good boat might be the leader for the spring hunt. When the hunt ended, so did that leader's responsibilities. Leaders were almost always men.

The adults in a band of several families chose leaders. The members of the band agreed to abide by a leader's decisions, which might include deciding when to move households and how the meat from a hunt should be divided among families.

▼ A model of an **umiak** (*OO mee ak*) made around 1880. The Inuit used this type of boat to hunt such large sea mammals as whales. The owner of such a boat would become the leader of the hunt. It would be his responsibility to decide on the best strategy for finding and killing a whale and to direct the other members of his crew. The crew agreed to abide by the leader's decisions for as long as the whale hunt lasted.

▲ Women carrying a seal hunter's catch. The Arctic and Subarctic peoples often chose a leader for a hunt. This would be a temporary position of authority. After a successful hunt, the leader decided how the meat would be divided among the members of the band.

SELECTING A CHIEF

The Aleuts were unusual in that they elected chiefs from the highest-ranking people in their society, the *honorables*. The Aleuts had war chiefs who led raiding parties against other villages. They also had peace chiefs who acted to protect the welfare of everyone in the village. Village representatives joined together to select the chiefs.

The Arctic and Subarctic peoples valued each person's right to make decisions for himself or herself. If one or more people disagreed with the leader's decisions, they could move to another band. In this way, people could avoid conflicts and personality clashes.

Elder Wisdom

The oldest people in a band were unlikely to participate in such physical activities as hunting. However, leaders viewed the band's **elders** with respect and often asked for their advice. The advice was especially helpful in trying to settle disputes that threatened to upset the stability of the band.

SOLVING PROBLEMS

The Arctic and Subarctic peoples had no written rules or books of law. Instead, survival depended on learning traditions and values passed from generation to generation. Each person was responsible for his or her own behavior and learned early in life that individual actions always had some type of impact on the group as a whole. For that reason, the Arctic and Subarctic peoples developed a number of ways to deal with people who threatened to endanger the community.

Ridicule

Among the Inuit, one way to punish an offender was to make fun of the person who behaved badly. The whole community teased the person or made jokes about him or her. They might also publicly gossip to try to embarrass the offender, shaming him or her into acting properly. In a small community where everyone knew everyone else, it was hard to ignore ridicule from one's friends and family.

SONG DUEL

Some Inuit groups handled conflict between two people by having a song duel. Each side of the argument composed insulting songs about the other person. If two men argued, their wives learned the songs as well. The two sides then sang their songs and danced in front of the whole community. The songs were often humorous. The person whose song got the best response from the crowd won the duel, and the conflict was resolved.

Wrestling

Many tribes used physical contests as a method of solving disputes. Wrestling matches were popular ways to settle a conflict. Usually, the wrestling match would take place in front of the people of the community. The person who won the match was seen to have superior strength, and the dispute was resolved in his favor.

Serious Trouble

When a person did something that was considered a serious offense, the consequences were serious as well. Often, the offending behavior was something that put the whole community in danger. This might involve starting a fight with another **band** or killing a

person within the community itself. **Banishment** was one of the most serious punishments. The offender was sent away from the community and not allowed to return. This was extremely dangerous for the offender because he or she had to live without the help of family and friends in the harsh Arctic or Subarctic environment. This punishment of banishment could be for a certain period of time. There were occasions, however, when a person was banished forever. The **elders** and other adults of the community met in public and discussed punishment for an offense before making a group decision.

▲ One of the most severe forms of punishment in Inuit society was banishment. Surviving for very long without the shared skills and communal help of the group was very difficult.

CONFLICT

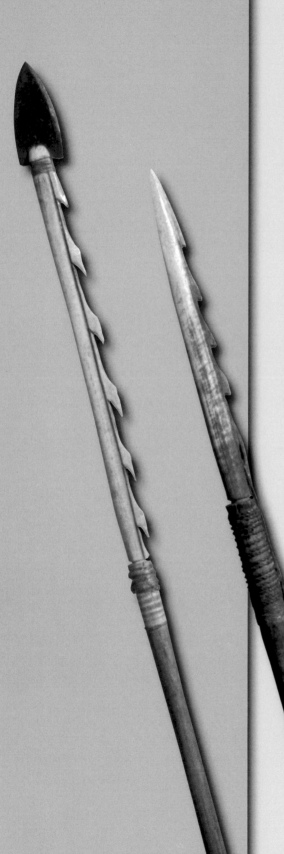

For the most part, the tribes and peoples of the Arctic and Subarctic were more likely to try to cooperate than engage in conflict. Bonds of kinship extended out to far-flung communities. It was not uncommon for several **bands** in a territory to have relationships with each other based on marriages, adoptions of orphans, or trade. Where these bonds existed, people shared possessions and food. Among some Inuit, people within a band might look down upon a man who had more animal skins or tools than he and his family could use. Those who had a great deal were expected to share that wealth with others.

Violence

Sometimes, however, cooperation failed. Protecting one's hunting and fishing grounds could mean the difference between life and death. A person might feel justified in killing someone from another band caught hunting or fishing on the person's land. Among some groups, the killing of a person, even by accident, warranted a violent response. The family and friends of the murdered trespasser might then respond by raiding the killer's village. Even personal disputes could erupt into full-scale war.

In war, the people of the Arctic and Subarctic often used the same **barbed** arrows and spears that they employed to hunt. The Aleuts even used the poison they used to hunt whales (see page 39) in combat with other Aleuts.

◀ Barbed arrows made by the Tanaina Indians of Alaska in the early 1800's. Used to hunt land and sea animals, they were also used as weapons against enemies. Disagreements over the right to hunt or fish in a certain area could trigger bloody raids between neighboring bands.

CONFLICT WITH VIKINGS

The Vikings who settled on Greenland and in Newfoundland around A.D. 1000 called the native people they encountered **skraelings** *(SKRAY lihngz)*. Experts are unsure of the origin of the term, but it may have meant something like **barbarian. Archaeologists** believe the Vikings were describing encounters with the ancestors of the Inuit. According to contemporary accounts by the Vikings, the skraelings were wary of the Norse, and the two **cultures** fought brutal battles. For the Inuit and the Subarctic peoples, control of natural resources was crucial to survival. Some archaeologists believe that they may have been defending their land from the Vikings to ensure their own survival. Eventually, after a number of violent conflicts, the Vikings left Newfoundland, though their descendants remained in Greenland until about the 1400's.

▲ L'Anse aux Meadows National Historic Site, in Newfoundland, is a re-creation of the Viking settlement established there around A.D. 1000. Conflicts with the native peoples led the Vikings to abandon the site, which was the first European settlement in North America.

THE SPIRIT WORLD

The spirit world was very real for Arctic and Subarctic peoples. To them, almost all things possessed a spirit or a soul. The Inuit believed that specially carved charms, or **amulets** *(AM yuh lihtz)*, had spirits of their own and could help the wearer during a hunt or protect the wearer from harmful spirits. Amulets were usually carved from ivory or bone and were attached to clothing.

Human beings and animals were believed to have souls. The Inuit of the central Arctic believed each animal had one soul. Human beings, however, could have several. These included the soul associated with a name inherited from an ancestor; the individual's soul that represented the breath of life; and the soul associated with the individual's body.

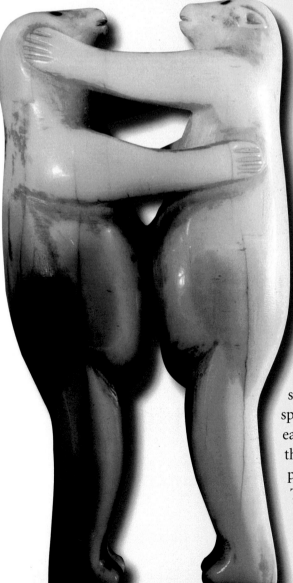

▼ An ivory Inuit amulet, carved in the 1800's, of two polar bears wrestling. People carried or wore amulets like this for protection from spirits.

Spirits of Good and Evil

The Algonquian-speaking people of the eastern Subarctic believed in an all-powerful spirit called Manitou *(MAN uh too)*. Manitou influenced every part of the Indians' lives. They also believed in individual spirits that were part of the land, such as water and tree spirits. The Inuit and the Athabaskan-speaking tribes believed in individual spirits associated with the natural world. For example, the Netsilik *(NEHT suh lihk)* Inuit of the Arctic believed in the goddess Nuliayuk *(noo lee AH yook)*, who lived at the bottom of the sea. They believed that Nuliayuk was the mother of all land and sea mammals. In addition to the spirits that helped or harmed people in general, the Inuit and Athabaskans also believed in personal guardian spirits. These were special spirits that each person had and that acted to help the person have a good life. There were also spirits that wanted to harm

WHALE REPORTS

The Inuit believed that the spirits of whales killed during a hunt returned to their homes in the sea and reported on how respectfully a slain whale had been treated. If the report was positive, the next spring whale hunt would be good because the whales were willing to once again offer themselves to the hunters.

people. The Subarctic Algonquian Indians believed that monsters called windigos *(WIHN dih gohz)* ate people and then spat them out. The people they spat out became cannibals who ate other human beings. Some Inuit feared giants and dwarfs that could eat whole caribou.

The Soul's Travels

Arctic and Subarctic peoples believed that a human soul lived on after the body had died. Some tribes believed that the soul stayed near the body for a while after death. The soul would then make its journey to a new life in a spiritual world or come back to Earth in a new body. Often, that body would be that of an animal. Many Inuit believed that a human soul passed through many animal lives before it became a human being once again. The soul might also be reborn in the next child in the family of the person who

had just died. An Inuit child could be called "Grandmother" or "Father" by older relatives because of this belief.

Animal Spirits

Animals were often called "animal persons" or "animal people" by the Arctic and Subarctic peoples. Some Athabaskan tribes believed that, at one time, human beings and animals spoke the same language. Animal souls, or spirits, were believed to have great power and were treated both with respect and fear. It was believed that the animals that were hunted willingly gave up their lives for the sake of humans. The animal spirits, therefore, had to be honored with gifts or special ceremonies. If the animal spirits were insulted, they might cause damage to the hunter's boat or weapons. Worse, they might stay out of sight, and the hunter's efforts to find food would fail.

◄ A hunting hat that may have been worn by an Aleut man of high standing in the early 1800's. The hat is painted with a bird design, and the long visor was intended to make the wearer appear birdlike. The carved ivory amulets that decorate the hat were intended to please the spirits of the animals that were being hunted. The hope was that if the hunted animal was pleased, it would allow itself to be taken. Each sea lion whisker at the back of the hat represented a successful hunt.

SHAMANS—LINKS TO THE SPIRITS

A shaman *(SHAH muhn)* was a man or woman who acted as a link between the world of human beings and the world of the spirits. A shaman was a powerful member of a **band** and had important responsibilities.

PROVING THEIR POWER

Shamans among some Subarctic Indian tribes, including the Cree and Naskapi, proved their power with a special ceremony called the tent-shaking ceremony. A shaman was bound with cords and placed inside a small tent. The rest of the band or group waited outside. Soon, the tent would shake violently and strange noises could be heard. The noises sounded like different birds or other animals, which the Indians believed were the voices of the spirits speaking to the shaman. When the shaking stopped, the shaman would appear outside the tent no longer tied up. He or she then related the messages of the spirits to the waiting people.

Finding Power

Shamans were believed to have acquired their power from spirits who appeared to them in dreams. Most people who wanted to become shamans started early in life. As young people, they became **apprentices** to an established shaman. Under the shaman's direction, a young person spent a great deal of time alone. He or she **fasted,** which led to trances or visions during which the spirits were said to make themselves known. The Arctic and Subarctic peoples believed that

▶ A wooden carving depicts two animal spirits helping an Inuit shaman during a trance. The shaman's drum lies next to him. Shamans often beat the drum in a slow and steady rhythm to help call the spirits.

once a shaman grew into adulthood, he or she continued this contact with the spirit world, which was the source of the shaman's power.

Explaining the Mysteries

A shaman's responsibilities included helping people understand the mysteries of life by acting as an interpreter between the spirit world and the human world. The shaman was believed to be able to speak to the spirits to find out why a hunting season had gone poorly or why a person had died. Breaking **taboos** *(tuh BOOZ)* and angering the spirits were believed to be the causes of many problems.

Curing Illness

One of the most important of a shaman's roles among the Arctic and Subarctic peoples was to cure illnesses. It was believed that illness occurred because an evil spirit entered a person's body or because the person's soul had left and was wandering. A shaman had several ways of handling this. He or she might have the sick person go through a sweating bath to get rid of the evil spirit. The shaman might also perform a **ritual** in which he or she was seen to suck the harmful spirit out of the sick person. The shaman then spit out shells or bits of bone as proof that the spirit had left.

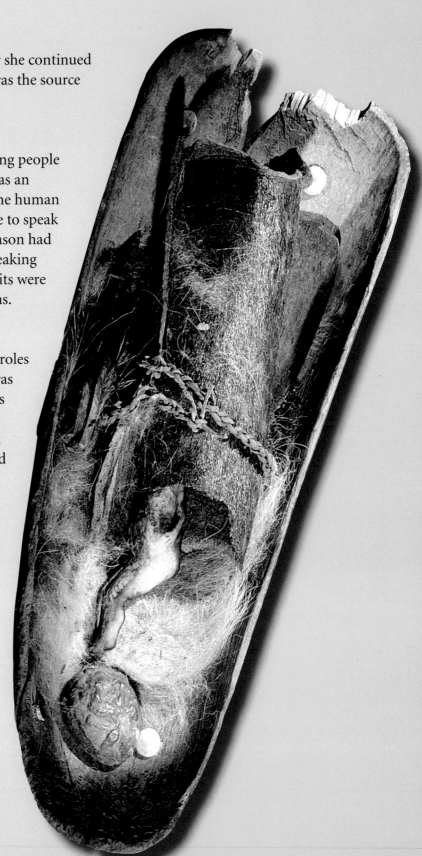

▶ A wooden Inuit bowl dating from about A.D. 100. The bowl holds some of the items a shaman might have used in a healing ceremony. The small, carved ivory figure depicts a seal or walrus. Arctic and Subarctic peoples believed that illnesses were caused by evil spirits in the body. The shaman might call on the spirit of the sea mammal to help him draw the evil spirit out of an ailing person.

TABOOS

Taboos are behaviors that are prohibited in a society. The Arctic and Subarctic peoples had many taboos that they observed to avoid illness or misfortune.

Avoiding Trouble with Animal Spirits

Keeping animal spirits content and willing to offer themselves as food was a great concern for all the people. Without the cooperation of the animals, the people would starve. Each animal had its own quirks that had to be recognized and respected. The Naskapi took great care to make sure that their dogs did not chew the bones from beavers they had killed. The Indians believed that the living beavers would be insulted and refuse to allow themselves to be killed in the future.

Caribou were so important to so many of the Arctic and Subarctic peoples that they received special attention. Women would wait until a hunt ended and the caribou herd had moved off before scraping the skin of a killed caribou. This was so that the living caribou would not see human beings causing suffering to one of their own kind.

▼ Caribou held a special place in the lives of the Arctic and Subarctic peoples. The peoples' survival was so greatly dependent on caribou that they held many taboos concerning the things that should or should not be done before, during, and after a hunt. The taboos were intended to keep the caribou pleased enough to allow themselves to be killed.

The Inuit believed that land and sea animals did not like each other. Because of this, caribou and seal meat were never cooked in the same pot. Only oil made from **blubber** (the fat of whales or other sea mammals) could be used to cook sea mammal meat. Hunters did not even eat caribou meat on the day they hunted seals. Women did not use the skins of sea and land animals in the same piece of clothing.

Taboos among People

There were also taboos that addressed aspects of life other than hunting, particularly childbirth and womanhood. Many Inuit considered it taboo to say the name of a deceased person until that name was given again to a newborn child. Even though women were considered important partners in day-to-day living, they were expected to follow certain **rituals** to avoid upsetting spirits. Hunters did not make eye contact with women in the period before the hunt, as it was believed that the hunter's keen eyesight would be harmed.

▼ A float rack meant to be mounted on a **kayak** *(KY ak)*, a narrow one-person boat. The Inuit used racks like this to hold such hunting tools as **harpoons,** spears, floats, and lines. The ivory seal figures are meant to please the seals being hunted. It was considered taboo to use items intended to hunt seals for the hunting of other animals, as it could offend the seals.

CEREMONIES AND CELEBRATIONS

The harsh climate of the Arctic and Subarctic discouraged many large outdoor celebrations. However, at particular times of the year, the people gathered for festivals and feasts.

Bladder Festival

The bladder festival was a celebration of the natural cycle of life—birth, death, and rebirth. Inuit hunters kept and preserved the bladders of the walruses, seals, and other sea mammals they had killed during the year. The Inuit believed that the spirits of the animals lived in the bladders.

▼ Sealskin gloves decorated with the beaks of puffins, sea birds that feed primarily by diving. Aleut and Inuit men wore such gloves while dancing in ceremonies. They would keep time to the beating of a drum by shaking the gloves, which would cause the beaks to rattle.

ALEUT MUMMIES

One Aleut funeral rite involved **mummifying** the body of an *honorable*, or person of the highest rank. The body was mummified by first removing the heart, stomach, lungs, and other internal organs. Next the emptied area was stuffed with dried grass. The body was then placed in a swift-moving stream. The constant running of the water slowly dissolved the fat in the body and washed it away. At the end of this process only skin, muscle, and the skeleton remained. The body was put in a sitting position and left out in the open air to dry. Once the body had dried, it was wrapped in leather and placed in a box along with the deceased person's favorite possessions. The box was usually placed on a platform in a cave. **Archaeologists** have found Aleut mummies more than 250 years old.

The bladders were inflated and decorated with paints, then hung in a **communal** building where everyone could see them. After the celebrations and feasting honoring the spirits, the bladders were returned to the sea. It was hoped the spirits would tell the living animals how well they had been treated.

Animal Ceremonies

The Subarctic Innu *(IHN noo)* people had a special feast called the Mokushan *(MAHK uh shahn)* that honored the caribou. Treating the bones of an animal in what was considered a proper way was an expression of respect. During the Mokushan feast, the community **elders** ate caribou fat and the marrow from caribou bones. Afterward, they beat drums and sang songs to honor the caribou spirits. Sometimes the bones were burned in a sacred fire.

The Deg Hit'an *(dehg HIHT uhn)* tribe of central Alaska performed an animal mask dance during the winter. Dancers wore carved masks representing different animals and people. The performances symbolized the interaction between hunters and animals and were done to increase the supply of game.

The Messenger Feast

The Inuit of northern Alaska had a ceremonial gathering called the messenger feast. It was usually held late in January, with one village hosting visitors from neighboring villages. The feast gets its name from the custom of sending messengers to villages to invite the community to the feast. The host village had gifts for the visitors, and the visitors brought gifts for the hosts. The messenger feast helped communities renew their ties with each other and promoted a spirit of cooperation.

MARRIAGE

The family was the focus of the Arctic and Subarctic peoples' lives. Survival depended on families working together. Marriage happened early in life, and children were considered the wealth of all the people.

Choosing a Mate

Most girls were married at age 14, but some girls married even younger. For boys, the average age was anywhere from about 16 to 20. Marriages were often arranged by the parents. In some cases, wedding plans were made before the children were even born or while they were still infants. Marriages arranged in this fashion reflected the desire of the parents to strengthen bonds between families.

In marriages that were not arranged, a young man courted a young woman for about a year. During this time, the young man might live with the girl's family. This would give him the opportunity to prove his worth as a hunter and provider. If all went well, the couple left to join the boy's family, at which point they would be considered married.

There were not always an even number of marriageable males and females. A good hunter might have two or more wives. Sometimes a man married two sisters and provided for both of them and all their children.

The relationship between man and wife was one of mutual respect and dependence. Even though the husband generally made such large family decisions as when to join a different **band**, the wife's opinion usually greatly influenced that decision. The goal in all relationships was to keep the family stable and free from conflict.

Joined Families

Sometimes the smallest band was simply one extended family. The feeling of closeness was often extended when two families that were particularly good friends would share one home. They would share food and possessions as if they were one family. They also shared responsibility for each other's well-being. All the married men shared the responsibility of caring for all the wives and children. If one of the men was killed, the remaining men in the family would provide for his wife and children.

MARRIAGE RESTRICTIONS

The peoples of the Arctic and Subarctic often had restrictions to prevent people who were considered too closely related from marrying. Among some Inuit, first cousins were considered too close; in some Subarctic Indian tribes, people within the same band were even thought to be too closely related to marry.

▶ An Inuit couple, photographed in the early 1900's. Traditionally, among the Arctic and Subarctic peoples, girls married very young— often by around 14 years of age. Boys usually married when they were between 16 and 20.

"Happy Jack" and Wife

LEARNING TRADITIONS

Children were very important to Arctic and Subarctic peoples and were well cared for. Childhood itself was very short, ending at **puberty**. Until then, children were expected to enjoy the freedom to learn and play.

Following the Leader

In most cases, children learned about life by imitating their **elders**. An older woman might spend time with a girl teaching her whatever the child wanted to learn. An older man would do the same with a young boy. The lessons lasted only as long as the child was interested. Many times the lessons were games that also taught skills. Boys made small versions of hunting weapons, and girls fashioned clothing and shoes for their dolls. The dolls were made of such material as wood or bone, which was carved into a human likeness. Plant fibers or even human hair was used for doll hair.

As children grew, they remained free to play, but they also started to take responsibility for chores and participating in adult activities. Boys as young as 8 accompanied their fathers on hunts. Girls learned from the women in their households and helped with butchering, preparing skins, and making clothing. Girls also learned the all-important skills of cooking and preserving food.

Children learned proper behavior as well from their elders. They learned such valued social rules as generosity and self-control. They also learned the importance of commitment to the welfare of the community. Each day brought new information about rules and **taboos** that shaped them as members of their community.

▲ Tagish Indian dolls dressed in clothing similar to what the children themselves would have worn. Children played with dolls carved from wood or bone.

Stories

Throughout the long winter, children learned traditions through stories told by adults. The oldest members of a family were highly esteemed for their knowledge. This knowledge was passed on in tales of adventure, past hunts, and the workings of the animal spirits. The stories also served to explain things in nature such as the **constellations** *(KON stuh LAY shuhnz)* or the **aurora borealis** *(aw RAWR uh BAWR ee AL ihs)*, the natural display of light in the sky also known as the northern lights. According to some stories, the sky is a hard dome stretched over the Earth. There is a hole in the dome through which spirits can pass to the next life, but the way is difficult to find. The spirits that live outside the dome light torches, so that spirits newly arriving can see where the hole is. The torches are the colors of the aurora borealis.

STORIES IN THE STARS

Animals and the hunt were so important to the peoples of the Arctic and Subarctic that they saw the star constellations as stories of different hunts. For example, the Big Dipper was not thought of as a giant ladle. Instead, it was seen as hunters pursuing an elk or a bear. The stars in the "handle" were the hunters, and the "bowl" of the dipper was the animal.

▼ The lights of the aurora borealis inspired many stories among the Arctic and Subarctic peoples. The Inuit of the lower Yukon River believed that the lights were the dancing souls of such animals as seals, deer, salmon, and beluga whales.

FOOD IN THE ARCTIC AND SUBARCTIC

The major staples of the diet for the peoples of the Arctic and Subarctic were meat and fish. However, during summer, Subarctic Indians collected berries and other plant foods. Berry-producing shrubs were important sources of food both for the Subarctic Indians and for the animals they hunted.

Available Resources

The Inuit and Subarctic Indians hunted many different animals. Fish was an important part of the diet for most Subarctic peoples, especially for those Athabaskans who lived on western salmon rivers. The Cree tribes hunted moose in the heavily forested areas in the southern Subarctic. In the northern Subarctic, the tribes followed the caribou. Large animals were not the only prey, though. Subarctic Indians also hunted snowshoe hares, porcupines, and squirrels. In the eastern Subarctic, beaver was an important source of food. The Netsilik Inuit hunted musk oxen, a large, hairy wild ox that lives in the Arctic. Most other Arctic people relied mainly on such sea mammals as seals, walruses, and whales.

The Inuit and Subarctic Indians ate every part of the animal that they could. Such internal organs as the liver and heart were favored foods. Soup could be made from blood. Leg bones were

▲ Arctic peoples such as the Netsilik Inuit hunted the musk oxen that lived on the Arctic **tundra.** An adult musk ox can grow to be 6 feet (2 meters) at the shoulders and weigh as much as 1,000 pounds (450 kilograms). An animal of this size provided Inuit hunters with a great deal of meat.

FAST FOOD

Pemmican (*PEHM uh kuhn*) was the traditional "fast food" for many Subarctic Indian tribes. Pemmican consisted of meat that had been dried, ground into a powder, then mixed with dried berries and animal fat. The result could be cut into strips or rolled into small balls. Pemmican was nourishing, easy to carry, and lasted as long as a year.

cracked for the marrow inside. The skin of fish was eaten along with the flesh.

Preparation

In the far north, much of the food was eaten raw. The main reason was lack of fuel to cook food. Wood was scarce, and using sea mammal oil for cooking used up the supply too quickly. If the choice was between staying warm with limited supplies of seal oil or having cooked food, most people chose to stay warm.

When food was cooked, it was usually boiled in containers made of animal skin or tree bark. Hot stones were placed in a container to heat the liquid. The Subarctic Indians also roasted or smoked meat and fish.

Storing food was extremely important to prevent starvation over the long winters. Meat and fish could be stored in **caches** (*KASH uhz*) located throughout a **band's** territory. These caches were pits in the ground or bags covered with heavy boulders. Winter meat could be kept frozen, but meat and fish caught in the summer months were preserved by drying. In the Arctic, where the summer weather brought little or no rainfall, people dried food on racks made of whalebones. Many Subarctic Indians dried meat on racks made of willow or other wood. People also dried meat and fish by hanging it over a smoking fire. The Aleuts built separate small buildings specifically as smokehouses.

▼ A photograph from 1928 of whale meat put out to dry in Alaska. Drying meat was a practical way to keep it from spoiling. Strips of whale, caribou, seal, or fish meat were hung from tall wooden racks, allowing the air and sun to slowly dry the meat. In areas where wood was scarce, whalebones were used to make the racks. Removing moisture from meat preserves it for a longer period of time.

COMMUNAL HUNTS

The large summer **migrations** of caribou, bowhead whales, and a variety of birds encouraged annual **communal** hunts. During these hunts, people from several **bands** joined together to try to kill as much prey as they could. Afterward, everything was divided up among those who had participated in the hunt. The choicest pieces of caribou, such as the tongue and nose, went to the man who made the first kill.

Caribou

For most Subarctic Indians, caribou was the main food source. Successful caribou hunting was, therefore, essential. Communal caribou hunts were common and were done in a number of ways. One method was called the *chute and pound*. The pound was a large, circular enclosure of mazes made of brush hedges. Snares were also tied to poles or tree stumps. The chutes were made of poles or other decoys that looked human to the frightened caribou. The decoys were positioned so that as the caribou moved away from them, they were herded into the pound, where waiting hunters killed them. Indians also hunted caribou from canoes, killing the animals as they crossed rivers or streams after being chased by another group of hunters.

Whale Hunt

A single bowhead whale could provide several tons of food. However, hunting and butchering a whale is a big job that requires a lot of people. In northern Alaska, the Inuit gathered along the coast and set up temporary camps to watch for the spring migration of the whales moving into the cold northern waters in order to feed.

When hunters spotted a whale, from four to eight men headed out into the water in a boat called an **umiak**. In most cases, the crew included the owner of the boat, a harpooner, and people to paddle the boat. The harpooner sat in the front of the boat, ready to throw the **harpoon**. The paddlers tried to get the umiak as close to the whale as possible, so that the harpooner could get a clear shot. The harpooner used a special type of harpoon that had air-filled sealskin bags attached to it. The harpoon head stuck and twisted into the flesh of an animal. The head then separated from the rest of the harpoon, but long leather thongs attached to the head prevented the animal from escaping. The air-filled bags made it hard for the whale to dive under water. Eventually the

◀ A harpoon made of wood, bone, ivory, iron, leather, and **sinew** used by the Inuit to hunt walruses. Before the Inuit came into contact with European traders, the harpoon head would not have had an iron blade.

whale tired and could be killed with a spear. Several more umiak crews helped tow the whale to shore, where it was butchered and divided up.

Today, Inuit whalers use many of the same techniques and materials that their ancestors did. Some present-day whalers have replaced the traditional umiak with more modern boats.

▼ An artist's impression of an Inuit whale hunt. Whale hunting was a dangerous activity that required many people working together. The paddlers in the umiak (the boat) tried to get as close to the animal as possible, to give the harpooner the best chance of success when he threw his harpoon. The water would be frigid, so staying warm meant staying dry. The hunters' outer parkas, mittens, and boots were made of stretched seal intestines, which were waterproof.

HUNTING WITH POISON
Some Aleuts hunted whales with harpoons fitted with a chipped stone blade that had been smeared with poison from the aconite *(AK uh nyt)* plant. The Aleuts made the poison by drying aconite root, then pounding or grating it. The root was soaked in water until it underwent a chemical change. At this point, it was applied to a harpoon. A poisoned harpoon blade killed the whale. The whale then drifted to shore, where the Aleuts butchered the animal. They were very careful to cut away the poisoned flesh from all around the harpoon blade so that it would not be eaten.

ARCTIC HOMES

▲ A 1926 photo of Inuit women building a snow igloo. The dense blocks of snow kept out cold and wind. It was important to properly shape the blocks when cutting them and to stack the blocks tightly. A long, slightly curved snow knife is used to make it easier to smooth snow over any small openings between the blocks, making the igloo as airtight as possible.

The main purpose of Arctic shelters was to protect people from wind and temperatures that could drop to -75 °F (-60 °C). Shelters might have to be constructed quickly in the case of sudden snowstorms or bitterly cold winds. Other shelters were part of semipermanent villages. Often, people built temporary shelters on the thick sea ice close to shore, where such sea mammals as walruses and seals could be hunted when they came up to breathe through holes in the ice.

Igloos

The word "igloo" often brings up a mental image of a domed house made of blocks of snow. While some igloos were made like this, there were other types of construction as well. It all depended on the situation in which the igloo was going to be used. In Arctic areas where there was little or no wood but plenty of hard-packed snow, igloos were made of blocks cut from the

SNOW PROBES

Some types of snow made better building blocks than other types. Snow forms in layers, and a snow block cut from more than one layer is likely to split apart. The best snow blocks were made from snow that was firm and uniform. To test the snow, some Arctic people used a tool called a snow probe. It was a long straight piece of antler or bone, from about 24 to 30 inches (about 60 to 75 centimeters) long. A man would push the snow probe slowly into a snowdrift. If the snow probe went in smoothly, the snow was likely to be one layer. If the probe seemed to hit hard and soft spots, it was likely the snow was in several layers and would not be good for cutting snow blocks. "Good" snow and "bad" snow might be only a few yards apart, so the igloo builder would use the probe to test different parts of a snowdrift.

snow with a special curved knife made of caribou antler or ivory. The blocks could be quickly assembled to provide a comfortably warm living space. A sheet of clear ice 3 to 4 inches (7.5 to 10 centimeters) thick was used as a window, allowing light to enter. It took a lot of fresh water to make an ice window. Fresh water was usually hard to find in the dry Arctic. Water from melted snow was usually reserved for drinking and cooking. Therefore, the inhabitants of the snow igloos would take the ice windows with them when they moved to another location. Sealskin or walrus gut was also used for windows. This type of window let in more light, but it was not as efficient as an ice window in preventing frigid air from getting into the igloo.

In other parts of the Arctic, igloos were made of a combination of materials, including driftwood, whalebone roof supports, boulders, sod, and animal skin. Stretched animal intestines were used for windows. All igloos had a tunnel at the entrance. The tunnel trapped cold air and prevented much of it from entering the living space. There might also be a curved wall in front of the tunnel entrance to prevent wind from whipping in.

Pit Houses

South Alaskan Inuit and the Aleuts built **pit houses** in their permanent winter villages. A village might have several pit-house homes for one or two families each and a larger **communal** pit house used for public gatherings. The base of the house was dug out of the ground. Above ground, the house had a frame of driftwood with sod walls. A roof opening allowed light to enter and smoke to escape. People entered the house through the roof opening and climbed down a notched log.

▼ A re-creation of an Inuit shelter built of driftwood covered with dirt and sod. Although wood was scarce in the Arctic, some wood might drift to shore from the sea. The dirt and sod act as a great natural barrier between cold outside air and the warmer air of the shelter. This type of shelter would likely have been part of a semipermanent winter or summer Inuit village.

SUBARCTIC HOMES

In most areas of the Subarctic, the Indians had to be on the move to find food, especially in the warmer months. Therefore, portability was an important feature of their homes. Winter homes, though, could be more permanent.

Winter Homes

For the Indians living in areas where wood was plentiful, a log home with a sod roof was a good choice for a winter home. These were rectangular and were made with logs covered with earth or snow. Each dwelling had a central fireplace and housed several related families. **Pit houses** were also common.

The **tipi** *(TEE pee)* was the most common type of shelter used by Subarctic Indians. A cone-shaped wooden frame was covered with tightly stitched caribou or moose skin. The fur side faced the inside of the tipi to keep warmth in and cold out. Some tipis had a covering made of sheets of birchbark.

Winter homes were usually part of a small village of several houses. Some villages had other special-use buildings, such as a place to smoke meat and fish and a **sweat lodge.** A sweat lodge was a small, low-roofed house where water was poured on hot stones to create steam. Men often used sweat lodges as part of a cleansing **ritual** between hunts.

Summer Homes

In the summer, portability was the most important feature of any shelter. The Indians were constantly moving to follow caribou herds and needed to be able to quickly set up shelter. Often, these hunting camps consisted of a series of shelters called **lean-tos** *(LEEN tooz)*. A lean-to consisted of a wood frame with an open end with either animal skin or pine boughs over it. They could be set up or taken down in minutes. Even though they were portable, the lean-tos offered a comfortable and protected area to eat and sleep.

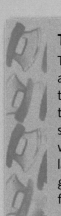

TRAVELING LIGHT
The skin coverings for tipis and lean-tos were often transported from one camp to another in canoes. The summer hunting camps were usually on rivers or lakes. This gave the Indians greater mobility in following game.

▶A tipi made with canvas cloth. Before interacting with European traders, Subarctic peoples used animal skin or birchbark to cover tipis. The sled to the side was used to transport the tipi and the family's goods.

CLOTHING IN THE ARCTIC

The Arctic's frigid winter temperatures and strong winds can freeze exposed skin in minutes. The people of the Arctic spent much of their time outdoors. For them, wearing the right clothing could mean the difference between life and death.

Efficient Protection

Inuit clothing was very efficient. It was important for people to be able to move around easily, so clothing had to be lightweight and comfortable. The extreme temperatures, of course, meant that clothing also had to be very warm. The Inuit achieved this balance of lightweight but warm by choosing the right materials for clothing and then wearing it in two layers. The clothing was also loose around the body but tight at neck and wrists. Keeping clothing loose around the body served two purposes: it made movement easier; and it allowed air warmed by body heat to circulate around the body. Keeping the clothing tight at neck and wrists helped keep that warm air from escaping or cold air from getting in. In warmer weather, the Inuit wore only one layer of clothing.

Most Inuit clothing was made from caribou skin or sealskin. Winter clothing worn next to the body would have the fur still on it. Skins such as caribou and seal are not **porous** *(PAWR uhs)*, so they trap the wearer's body heat. The hairs of the fur help circulate the body's heat, keeping the wearer warm but preventing dangerous overheating. A large fur ruff attached to a hood protected the face. Many tribes used wolverine fur because ice and frost do not stick to it.

Daily Clothes

Men, women, and children wore similar clothing—including double-layered pants, a knee-length coat with a hood, mittens, and tall boots called **mucklucks** *(MUHK luhkz)*. For extra warmth inside their boots, the Inuit wore socks woven from

◀ A 1903 photograph of an Inuit man wearing a sealskin coat. Since sealskin is not porous, that is, it doesn't allow much air to pass through it, it helps keep in body heat. The man wears sealskin boots that come up to his knee for extra warmth. Sealskin pants are tucked into the boots to prevent cold air from getting inside.

grass. Hunters who spent a lot of time in or near water wore clothing made of such waterproof material as the stretched intestines of seals and walruses. Women's clothing included a pouch on the back of the coat to carry a baby.

The Inuit made clothing that was beautiful as well as useful. They used **sinew** to stitch pieces of animal skin together. The clothing might be decorated by using different colored furs or by attaching colorful fur or animal-skin fringes. They attached shells or carved bone beads onto the clothing to create decorative designs.

Body Decorations

Inuit men and women used tattoos as a form of body decoration. Inuit women usually had three lines that ran from beneath the lower lip to the chin. Often, the women also had more detailed patterns on their arms or legs. At **puberty**, many Inuit boys and girls had a slit cut at either corner of their mouths under the lower lip. They would insert a bone or stone ornament called a **labret** (*LAY breht*) into each opening.

Sewing Kits

Getting caught out on the ice with a torn coat could be very dangerous. The Inuit carried sewing kits in pouches made of bird skin or fur. Each kit contained sinew, pieces of fur for repair, needles made out of bone, an **awl** (a sharp tool for making holes in leather or wood), and a thimble.

▼ Woven grass socks that were worn inside boots. The extra layer kept the feet warmer. The grass absorbed perspiration, keeping the wearer's feet drier.

CLOTHING IN THE SUBARCTIC

The clothing of the Subarctic Indians varied depending on where in this vast region the people lived. Some areas of the Subarctic border the Arctic, and weather conditions are very similar. Other areas of the Subarctic stretch much farther south. In these areas, winters could be fierce but summers were mild compared with Arctic summers.

People of the Pointed Skins

The northern Subarctic Indian tribes shared similar clothing styles with their Arctic Inuit neighbors. They wore layers of clothing made of caribou and other animal skins. These included a hooded overcoat, pants, mittens, and boots. Even though the basic types of clothing were similar, a tribe might have a particular style. For example, the Chipewyan were called the People of the Pointed Skins because of the style of their coats, which had long pointed tails in the front and back. Some tribes made soft and warm underclothes from the skins of snowshoe hares. Tribes that lived in Alaska and northern Canada decorated their clothing with fringe cut from animal skins or fur, caribou teeth, and feathers.

Southern Influence

The tribes that lived in the southern areas of the Subarctic wore warm clothing but also had the opportunity to wear lighter clothing during the brief summer months. Cree men and women wore tight-fitting leggings made of caribou or other animal skin, over which they wore long **tunics**. The tunic was an all-weather garment because it had sleeves

◀ A Cree woman's tunic. The Subarctic Indians wore short and long tunics made of animal skin, usually deer or caribou. In colder weather, sleeves could be attached to the tunic at the shoulders. Stitching together two different colored skins in a checkerboard or striped design was a popular way to decorate clothing. Fringe along the seams added to the beauty of the garment.

Two Years of Tattooing

Cree men and women tattooed their
hands, as well as parts of their faces
and sometimes other areas of the body,
as seen in the portrait of Cree Chief
Mahsette-Kui Uab at right. They usually
began the tattooing process about a
year before marriage. The highly detailed
tattoos were made by cutting into the
skin and then pressing **sinew** rubbed
in charcoal into the cuts. It was a
painful process that was repeated
to make new tattoos until about
a year after the marriage.

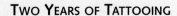

that could be removed in
warmer weather. In cold
weather, people wore
fur-lined caribou hats
or hoods to keep their heads
warm. In addition, they
sometimes decorated their
clothes with feathers and
porcupine quills and
trimmed garments with
beaver fur.

Footwear

Subarctic Indians favored caribou or moose-hide **moccasins**
for their footwear. Moccasins could be ankle-length for the
summer or knee-length for the colder seasons. For additional
warmth, people lined taller moccasins with the fur of rabbits or
ermines. (Ermines are members of the weasel family.) Besides
being comfortable and durable, moccasins had the advantage
of not damaging the bottoms of canoes or tearing through the
webbing on snowshoes.

DOGS IN THE ARCTIC AND SUBARCTIC

Dogs were a vital part of life for many Arctic and Subarctic peoples. Several different types of dogs were bred for specific jobs. Since there were no horses, dogs acted as pack animals. A strong dog could carry 20 to 25 pounds (9 to 11 kilograms) of goods on its back without much effort. Often, dogs carried much more weight than that. Dogs were also used as a means of transportation. Groups of dogs pulled light sleds with human passengers or heavier vehicles loaded with household goods. Some Inuit and Subarctic Indians used dogs to hunt.

Arctic Dogs

The qimmiq *(KIHM ihk)*, also known as the Canadian Inuit Dog or the Canadian Eskimo Dog, is large with a broad **muzzle**, thick fur, and a curled tail that looks similar to the Siberian husky or Alaskan malamute. Qimmiqs were valuable members of many Inuit villages. A family usually owned 4 to 6 dogs but sometimes had as many as 10. A person with 10 dogs was considered quite wealthy, as it was hard to keep that many dogs well fed.

Qimmiqs pulled sleds loaded with a hunter's freshly killed meat or pulled the type of large sled known as a **sledge** *(slehj)* loaded with household goods. Sometimes they pulled human passengers. These types of dogs

▲ A contemporary photo of an Inuit man and his dogs resting on Baffin Island in the Canadian territory of Nunavut *(NOO nuh voot)*. Like their human owners, dogs in the Arctic and Subarctic need to keep warm in very cold temperatures. The kind of dog traditionally used to pull sleds in the Arctic has two layers of fur: the soft undercoat helps to keep body heat in; the coarser outer coat helps keep the animal's skin dry. Many Arctic working dogs also had especially wide feet that allowed them to travel more efficiently on snow—something like natural snowshoes.

were very well trained. They had to be to avoid the temptation of eating the meat they were hauling. One dog out of the team of four or six would stand out as a leader. This dog was usually the strongest and the most willing to work. Some qimmiqs were talented seal hunters. They could sniff out the small breathing holes seals used even if those breathing holes were covered with snow.

Subarctic Hunting Dogs

The Cree and Chipewyan Indians used a type of dog that was smaller than the qimmiq. Some dog experts call this now **extinct** breed the Common Indian Dog. This type of dog was usually black or gray, and it had a narrower head than the qimmiq and longer legs. Although it sometimes pulled sleds, the Cree and Chipewyan mostly used this type of dog to carry packs and to hunt. In hunting, either a single dog accompanied a human hunter or packs of dogs were used to chase down game. The dogs also worked as camp watchdogs, alerting villagers to possible raids from other tribes or to the presence of a dangerous animal.

The Tahltan *(TAHL tuhn)* Indians used a small dog, weighing from 10 to 18 pounds (4.5 to 8 kilograms), to hunt everything from rabbits and **ptarmigans** *(TAHR muh guhnz)* to bears and lynxes. Even though this Tahltan Bear Dog was only about 12 to 16 inches (30 to 40 centimeters) tall at the shoulder, its energy and bravery made it a valuable companion. Its barking and quick movements around a large bear served to annoy the bear enough to keep it at bay until a hunter could arrive to kill the bear with an arrow or a spear. The Tahltan Bear Dog is now extinct.

DOGS IN THE SKY

The Inuit believed that the star cluster now called the Pleiades *(PLEE uh deez)*, in the **constellation** Taurus, came into being when a bear named Nanuk was attacked by a pack of fierce dogs. Nanuk tried to run away, but the dogs stayed close to him. Eventually, Nanuk and the dogs came to the edge of the world and fell off into the sky, where they became the stars that form the Pleiades.

ARCTIC TRAVEL

The Arctic peoples needed reliable ways to travel through their usually frozen environment. Even when winter camps were set up, hunters still needed to be able to move around to find game and bring home meat. They also needed to be able to move their families from one winter village to another. In parts of Alaska, the long dark winters were the time for the bladder festival and other celebrations (see page 30). In spring and fall, the Inuit traveled to meet others for **communal** hunts and to trade.

Land Travel

Most Arctic land travel was done on foot. Sometimes supplies were carried in packs strapped on the backs of people or dogs. Often, though, a team of dogs pulled the supplies on a large heavy sled called a **sledge**, which was usually made of wood or whalebone. A sledge might be as long as 20 to 30 feet (6 to 9 meters) and carry many hundreds of pounds. The runners of the sledge were covered with frozen mud that had been carefully smoothed with a knife, so that the sledge would slide easily over the ground. Between the slick runners and the traction of the dogs' claws,

▲ An Inuit man on his sled on Baffin Island in Nunavut in a contemporary photo. Using a strong sled that would be pulled by dogs was the easiest way to move supplies or other heavy items overland in the Arctic.

▼ An Inuit man in a kayak, the most common type of boat used by Arctic peoples, near Nome, Alaska, in a 1914 photo. The boat's design keeps it low into the water and, therefore, unlikely to capsize, or turn over— an important feature in frigid waters.

an Arctic traveler could move heavy loads many miles. A person ran behind the sledge or off to the side of it to guide the dogs.

Water Travel

For travel in coastal waters, the Arctic people used a **kayak**, a narrow one-person boat made of sealskin stretched over a frame of wood or bone. The sealskin covered the top of the boat, except for a hole in the middle where the person sat. A double-bladed paddle was used to move and steer the boat. Kayaks were used to hunt such sea mammals as seals and otters. Hunters also used kayaks in rivers and lakes to hunt caribou. **Umiaks** were larger, skin-covered boats that could carry several people or a load of household goods. They were also used to hunt whales.

Among the Aleuts, women were responsible for covering the larger boats with sea lion skins. It was considered very important that none of the women's hair got caught in the seams. The Aleuts believed that the presence of the hair would anger a sea lion, who would see the hair as a contamination. The angry sea lion would then bite a hole in the boat.

SUBARCTIC TRAVEL

The Indians in the most northern parts of the Subarctic, such as the Deg Hit'an, used similar methods of travel as their Inuit neighbors. Other Subarctic Indians developed unique transportation methods that suited their specific winter and summer travel needs.

Snow, Snow, Snow

Snow in all its many forms was a travel challenge throughout the Subarctic. When people traveled on foot, snowshoes were the most popular travel aid. They were made in many different shapes and sizes to suit the type of land on which they would be used. When they needed to move larger loads, the Subarctic Indians used **toboggans** made of thin wooden boards. The front of the toboggan curved upward to make it easier to move through deep snow. Lightweight sleds were used on hard-frozen ground or lake surfaces. They had long, narrow runners that allowed the sled to move quickly over slick surfaces.

Land of Lakes and Rivers

During the warmer months, the ground in the Subarctic was often too soggy to allow people to move comfortably over land for any great distance. Therefore, the Subarctic Indians did most of their traveling by boat. The most common kind of boat was the canoe, which consisted of a wooden frame covered with caribou hide. Some of the Algonquian-speaking tribes used sheets of birchbark. The hide or bark was stitched together with **sinew**, then sealed with boiled **resin** from pine or spruce trees to make the canoe waterproof. Birchbark canoes were valued because they were very light, making them easy to carry overland from one waterway to another. Some of the Athabaskan tribes also used larger, heavier canoes covered in sturdy moose hide. These canoes were large enough to carry several families and their household goods. The Cree built what they called a "crooked canoe." The hull was slightly flared and twice as high as a standard canoe hull. The crooked canoe was very stable and easy to steer in rivers and in swirling river rapids.

▶ The birchbark canoe was particularly useful to Subarctic Indians because it was very light, making it easy to carry overland between bodies of water.

TUMPLINES

Indians often had to rely only on themselves to carry large objects over many miles. One way of doing this was to use a strap called a tumpline. A single long cord was attached to a rolled bundle carried on a person's back. Part of the loop ran up the carrier's back and across the forehead. A tumpline might also be used across a carrier's chest.

ENTERTAINMENT

Survival was such a constant challenge that many forms of entertainment for adults and children centered on developing skills that would help people meet that challenge. There were entertainments, though, that were just for fun.

Games of Skill

As with young children nearly everywhere, the children of the Arctic and Subarctic played with wooden dolls, tops, and carved animals. They listened to stories of adventure and narrow escapes from danger. However, no one ever forgot that living in the Arctic and Subarctic was physically demanding. When a chance came to have fun but also build strength and agility, that chance was quickly taken. For boys and men, such games as tug-of-war and wrestling were popular. An exciting game that consisted of trying to throw a dart through a rolling, webbed hoop was fun but also helped develop the skills needed to accurately throw a **harpoon** or spear in the hunt. The Cree played a ball game similar to **lacrosse** *(luh KRAWS)*. Girls played games that helped increase their skills in such traditional women's roles as food and animal skin preparation. Girls had smaller versions of the traditional **ulu.**

◀ Inuit children photographed on Nunivak Island, off the coast of Alaska, in 1929.

The Athabaskans in central Alaska enjoyed a game similar to modern ice hockey. A wooden block was buried in the middle of a field. Opposing teams raced to dig out the block, then used sticks to move it to the end of the other team's half of the playing field. In another game, a player tried to pull a moose skin from one point to another while other players tried to stop him by driving sticks into the skin. If the player pulling the skin succeeded, it was seen as a measure of that person's shrewdness and cleverness.

Music and Dancing

The peoples of the Arctic and Subarctic combined singing, dancing, and drumming at their celebrations. Drums were usually fairly big around but not very deep, looking like giant tambourines. The drumheads were made of stretched material, such as whale liver, walrus stomach, or caribou skin. The drums were struck with bone or ivory sticks.

The Inuit practiced a musical form called throat singing, which was often done to entertain children. Throat singers were usually two women who stood close to and facing each other. They tightened and released their abdominal muscles and breathed rapidly. This created a kind of buzzing sound. The two singers coordinated their movements to make it seem like there was one sound.

▲ Inuit drummers perform at a celebration using drums with heads made of stretched whale stomachs. The drummers would blend different beats and rhythms on the drums, encouraging listeners to join in the fun of the dance.

CHALLENGES TO TRADITION

When the peoples of the Arctic and Subarctic came into contact with European explorers, traders, and settlers, their traditional ways of life were changed forever. While some of the change was positive, much of it came at a very high cost.

Vikings (originally from Scandinavia in northern Europe) who had settled on Greenland arrived in Newfoundland, in eastern Canada, around A.D. 1000. For a time, they established a settlement there and had contact with the peoples living there. Unlike the Europeans who arrived centuries later, the Vikings had very little influence on the native peoples.

Search for the Northwest Passage
In 1576, the English explorer and navigator Martin Frobisher *(FROH bih shuhr)* arrived in

▲ A re-creation of a fur trader's cabin from the early 1800's at Fort William in Thunder Bay, Ontario. The scale in the foreground shows how **pelts** were weighed. Beaver pelts were stacked onto the scale until their weight was enough to lift the weighted cloth bag from the floor and to the same level as the furs. The arrival of European fur traders brought vast changes to the Arctic and Subarctic peoples' way of life.

North America to seek a Northwest Passage to India and eastern Asia. He ended his voyage in a body of water now known as Frobisher Bay, off what is now called Baffin Island in northeastern Canada. Here he traded with the Inuit before returning to England with news of the northern lands he had discovered.

Over the next 200 years, many other explorers tried—without success—to find a northern route to China, either sailing along Arctic coasts or traveling up Canadian rivers. Their expeditions brought them into contact with the native peoples, increased Europeans' knowledge of the region and its resources, and contributed to the growth of trade with the peoples of the Arctic and Subarctic.

Whalers and Fur Traders

Beginning in the late 1700's, European and American whalers began hunting in Arctic waters. They employed Inuit men for their whale hunts and traded with the Inuit for ivory and other items. Western European and Russian fur traders established trading outposts in many places throughout the Arctic and Subarctic. In exchange for the furs of **taiga** and **tundra** animals, the native peoples received such useful items of European technology as steel needles, knives, and axes—and also guns and alcohol. Most Inuit and Subarctic Indians were friendly to the whalers and fur traders they met. They appreciated the trade goods they received because those goods made life more pleasant. Unfortunately, there were sometimes violent encounters with the traders over alcohol or women. The traders also brought such European diseases as smallpox, influenza, measles, and tuberculosis (*too BUR kyuh LOH sihs*). The Arctic and Subarctic peoples had never been exposed to these diseases before and, therefore, had never built up a natural **immunity** to them. As a result, many people died.

▼ *Whaling in the Arctic*, a painting by the English artist Robert Willoughby (1768–1843). European whalers began hunting in the Arctic in the late 1700's. They valued the skills and knowledge of the Inuit and often hired them to help hunt whales.

LOOKING AHEAD

Today, many of the Arctic and Subarctic peoples are looking for ways to recapture the best of their traditions and integrate them into their modern lives.

Failed Treaties

Like other native peoples in North America, the Inuit and the Subarctic Indian tribes faced a series of broken agreements with those who followed the original Western European and Russian explorers and traders. European settlers followed the fur traders, and slowly the Arctic and Subarctic peoples lost more and more of their rights to the land and its resources. Colonists also brought cultural changes, forcing them on the Arctic and Subarctic peoples and leading to the loss of their traditional ways of life as well as their land. European **culture** stressed the rights of individuals and the idea of personal success and wealth. This contrasted sharply with the Arctic and Subarctic peoples' long tradition of cooperation.

The traders and settlers also brought new religious faiths and often forced their beliefs on the Inuit and Subarctic Indians. The earliest religious **missionaries** (*MIHSH uh NEHR eez*) sometimes treated the spiritual beliefs of the Arctic and Subarctic peoples with extreme disrespect. As more and more of North America was colonized, the

NUNAVUT

Nunavut is an Inuit word meaning *Our Land*. In 1993, the Canadian government passed legislation to create, out of the eastern portion of Canada's Northwest Territories, the new territory Nunavut. At the same time, another law gave the Inuit people exclusive ownership of about one-fifth of Nunavut's land. The new territory formally came into existence on April 1, 1999. Nunavut has a population that is 85 percent Inuit. The territory's legislature can pass laws governing local matters, and the existence of the territory gives the Inuit a dedicated space in which to live largely as they choose. Today, Nunavut is building its economy in a variety of areas that support a traditional Inuit value system. These areas include fishing, hunting, tourism, and traditional arts and crafts. Nunavut continues to face its own challenges in employment and government as it becomes a homeland within a homeland for the Inuit.

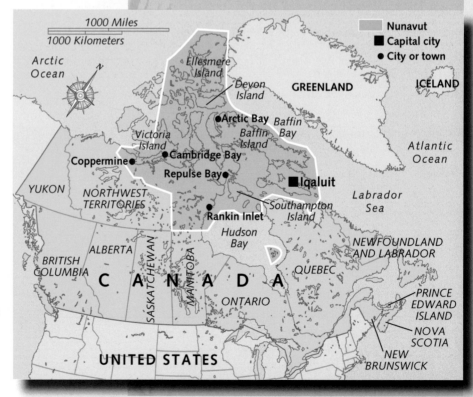

new governments continued to take away territory and rights from the original inhabitants of the land. The Arctic and Subarctic peoples found themselves barred from traditional hunting areas or prevented from moving freely within territory that had been theirs to roam for thousands of years. Increasingly, the Inuit and Subarctic Indians faced poverty and racial discrimination.

Modern Efforts

Beginning in the 1970's, the Inuit joined with other native peoples to try to improve their lives. They also began educational programs to help others better understand their cultures and traditions. In 1996, Nunavut Arctic College began a program called the Oral Traditions Project. The goal of the project was to talk to Inuit elders and record their stories and knowledge of Inuit history, so that the information could be preserved and passed on to future generations. The Inuit have also formed networks of support organizations to help their own people meet the challenges of modern life while still honoring their traditions. Using modern Internet technology, they are reaching out to native peoples throughout the region to educate and to support their growth into the future.

▶ Fireworks light up the sky at midnight on April 1, 1999, in Iqaluit *(ee KAH loo iht)* in celebration of the first day of existence of the new Canadian territory of Nunavut. Iqaluit is the territory's capital.

GLOSSARY

alliance A union formed by agreement, joining the interests of people or states.

amulet A charm worn to guard against evil.

apprentice A person who learns a trade by working under the guidance of a skilled master.

archaeologist A scientist who studies the remains of past human cultures.

aurora borealis The streamers or band of light appearing in the northern sky at night; northern lights.

awl A sharp-pointed tool used to punch small holes in such materials as leather and wood.

band A group of several extended families, related by blood or marriage, that lived in an area.

banish To condemn a person to leave a community; exile.

barbarian A person who is considered uncivilized.

barbed Having sharp backward-facing points.

blubber The fat of whales and some other sea animals.

cache A hiding place for food, supplies, or other important goods; also the goods themselves.

communal Something shared by a group.

constellation A group of stars, usually having a geometric shape within a definite region of the sky.

culture A society's arts, beliefs, customs, institutions, inventions, language, technology, and values.

deciduous Shedding leaves each year. Maples, elms, and most oaks are deciduous trees.

elder An older and more influential member of a tribe or community.

extinct Died out completely.

fast To go without food.

harpoon An arrow-shaped weapon used to spear large fish and such sea mammals as whales.

ice age A period in Earth's history when ice sheets cover vast regions of land.

immunity Resistance to disease.

kayak A light, narrow boat with a deck. The deck features an opening in which the kayaker sits.

labret A lip ornament.

lacrosse A team sport played with a ball and sticks with net pockets.

lean-to A shelter consisting of a covered frame, usually open on one of the long sides.

migrate To move from one place to another.

missionary A person who works to spread a religion.

moccasin A soft shoe, often made from the skin of an animal, and usually not having a heel.

muckluck A high, soft, waterproof, fur-lined boot often made of sealskin.

mummy A dead body that has been preserved and that still has some of its soft tissue—that is, a body that has decayed only to a limited degree. The preservation of the body may have been intentional, using artificial means, such as salts and resins. Or, the preservation may have been natural—for example, a body left in a dry, cold climate was sometimes naturally dried and preserved. In some cultures, both animals and people were mummified.

muzzle An animal's nose, mouth and jaws.

pelt The skin of an animal, with the fur still attached.

permafrost Ground that remains frozen for two or more years.

pit house An ancient house style, made by digging a hole in the ground and constructing a shelter over the pit.

porous Having many small holes that allow the movement of air or other gases.

ptarmigan A game bird with feathered feet often found in mountainous and cold regions.

puberty The physical beginning of manhood and womanhood.

resin A sticky substance that flows from some plants and trees.

ritual A solemn or important act or ceremony, often religious in nature.

shaman A person believed to have powers that come from direct contact with spirits.

sinew A tough, strong band or cord that joins muscle to bone; tendon.

skraeling The name the Vikings gave to the people they encountered on Greenland and in eastern Canada.

sledge A large sled used to transport heavy items.

sweat lodge A building heated so as to cause people inside it to perspire. Ceremonies held in a sweat lodge are used to purify the body, cure illnesses, and influence spirits.

taboo The system or act of setting things apart as forbidden.

taiga Swampy, evergreen forest land found in the Subarctic.

tipi A cone-shaped lodging made of poles covered with hides.

toboggan A long, flat sled with an upward-curving front.

tundra A vast, level, treeless plain in the Arctic regions.

tunic A loose, short piece of clothing that is slipped on over the head and is often belted at the waist.

ulu An Inuit knife with a flat curved blade, used for cutting animal skins and preparing food.

umiak An open boat, broader and longer than a **kayak,** used by the Inuit.

ADDITIONAL RESOURCES

Books

The Cree
by Raymond Bial (Benchmark Books, 2005)

The Gale Encyclopedia of Native American Tribes, Volume 3: Arctic, Subarctic, Great Plains, Plateau
edited by Sharon Malinowski and others
(Gale, 1998)

The Inuit
by Raymond Bial (Benchmark Books, 2002)

The Inuit
by Suzanne M. Williams (Franklin Watts, 2003)

Inuit Mythology
by Evelyn Wolfson (Enslow, 2001)

Native Tribes of the North and Northwest Coast
by Michael Johnson and Jane Burkinshaw
(World Almanac Library, 2004)

Web Sites

http://arcticcircle.uconn.edu/HistoryCulture/

http://www.mnh.si.edu/arctic/features/fisher/index.html

http://www.mnh.si.edu/arctic/features/yupik/index.html

http://www.native-languages.org/kids.htm

http://www.nmai.si.edu/subpage.cfm?subpage=exhibitions&second=dc&third=current

INDEX

Acknowledgments

The Art Archive: 6 (National Anthropological Museum, Mexico/Gianni Dagli Orti), 44, 51 (Culver Pictures); Bridgeman Art Library: 57 (Simon Carter Gallery, Woodbridge, Suffolk, UK); Canadian Museum of Civilization: 15, 22, 34, 46; Corbis: 5, 33 (Michael Maslan Historic Photographs), 9, 11, 28, 36 (Galen Rowell), 12 (Christopher Morris), 13, 41 (Marilyn Angel Wynn/Nativestock Pictures), 14 (PEMCO-Webster & Stevens Collection; Museum of History and Industry, Seattle), 19, 40 (Bettmann), 23 (Greg Probst), 37, 55 (no photographer credited), 43 (Abbie Enock, Travel Ink), 47 (Historical Picture Archive), 20–21, 48, 50 (Rob Howard), 49 (Stocktrek Images), 56 (Lowell Georgia); Getty Images: 59 (Carlo Allegri/AFP); Nativestock: 52–53 (Marilyn Angel Wynn); Shutterstock: 35 (Walter S. Becker); Werner Forman Archive: 1, 18, 27, 29 (Jeffrey F. Myers Collection), 7 (Haffenreffer Museum of Anthropology, Brown University, Rhode Island), 8 (no photographer credited), 17, 30 (Smithsonian Institution, Washington, D.C.), 24 (Alaska Gallery of Eskimo Art), 25 (The British Museum, London), 36 (National Museum, Denmark), 38, 45 (William Channing).

Cover image: Corbis (Rob Howard)
Back cover image: Shutterstock (Joop Snijder, Jr.)